I0492172

Business Process Outsourcing Unleashed

By Ade Asefeso MCIPS MBA

Copyright 2014 by Ade Asefeso MCIPS MBA
All rights reserved.

Second Edition

ISBN-13: 978-1499656244

ISBN-10: 1499656246

Publisher: AA Global Sourcing Ltd
Website: http://www.aaglobalsourcing.com

Table of Contents

Disclaimer

This publication is designed to provide competent and reliable information regarding the subject matter covered. However, it is sold with the understanding that the author and publisher are not engaged in rendering professional advice. The authors and publishers specifically disclaim any liability that is incurred from the use or application of contents of this book.

If you purchased this book without a cover you should be aware that this book may have been stolen property and reported as "unsold and destroyed" to the publisher. In this case neither the author nor the publisher has received any payment for this "stripped book."

Dedication

This book is dedicated to the hundreds of thousands of incredible souls in the world who have weathered through the up and down of recent recession.

To my family and friends who seems to have been sent here to teach me something about who I am supposed to be. They have nurtured me, challenged me, and even opposed me…. But at every juncture has taught me!

This book is dedicated to my lovely boys, Thomas, Michael and Karl. Teaching them to manage their finance will give them the lives they deserve. They have taught me more about life, presence, and energy management than anything I have done in my life.

Chapter 1: Understanding Outsourcing

Outsourcing is a term which has received a great deal of attention lately. Despite the increasing trend in companies relying on outsourcing there are still some who do not clearly understand what is meant by the term outsourcing. This book will examine some of the key elements of outsourcing to help the reader develop a better understanding of the concept of outsourcing.

Outsourcing Defined

What is outsourcing? This is the most basic question many have about the subject of outsourcing. They are not yet interested in more complex aspects of the issue because they have not yet grasped the most basic understanding of the process. In the simplest language outsourcing is when a company delegates the completion of certain tasks to an individual not employed by the company directly. This individual may be an independent contractor or an employee of another company who is subcontracted to complete these tasks. In exchange for the individual's services, he or his company receives monetary compensation.

This description of outsourcing makes it far easier to understand the concept. Most people incorrectly assume outsourcing only applies to situations where large corporations have products manufactured overseas by a subsidiary and don't realize examples of outsourcing can be seen just about everywhere in corporate America and UK.

Domestic Outsourcing

Domestic outsourcing refers to outsourcing where both the primary company and the independent contractor or subsidiary is located in the same country. One of the main reasons for outsourcing is to reduce costs but it is not always necessary to outsource work overseas to reduce costs. Cost savings will be discussed in greater detail in this book on the benefits of outsourcing but essentially outsourcing results in a savings as a result of a reduction of labour costs.

Overseas Outsourcing

Overseas outsourcing is the type of outsourcing most people already understand. This is where large corporations such as Nike, and even some smaller companies, employ manufacturing plants overseas in third world countries to upsize their profits. This is significant because their costs including wages, materials and building lease would be considerably higher in the United States and UK than they are in these other countries.

Benefits of Outsourcing

Now that you have a clearer understanding of the concept of outsourcing, you might wonder why companies would go to the trouble of outsourcing certain tasks. Outsourcing is popular because there are great deals of benefits to the companies who outsource the work. Some of the benefits include:

1. Reduced labour costs
2. Increased workforce
3. Greater flexibility

One of the main reasons companies resort to outsourcing is it can significantly reduce costs. In the case of overseas outsourcing of manufacturing tasks, costs can be cut dramatically because there are lower wages and costs associated with managing and maintaining the manufacturing plants. However, companies also enjoy a cost savings when they outsource tasks domestically. Reduction of labour costs is the primary source of savings in this case. Independent contractors hired on a contract basis for the purpose of completing specific tasks are often not given benefits such as social security, Medicare and workers compensation.

Another benefit to outsourcing is enjoying a larger workforce without actually hiring additional employees. Companies who maintain networking relationships with qualified individuals have more opportunities open to them because they are able to rely on these individuals to assist them if they acquire large or complicated projects.

Finally, outsourcing gives a company a great deal of flexibility. Companies who have a significant workload and backlog of work where the majority of the employees are highly utilized might be hesitant to compete for new work because they do not have a great deal of employee availability. However, with a network of individuals to rely on if the need to outsource arises, the company has more flexibility in pursuing new work.

Chapter 2: Outsourcing Today

Outsourcing has different dimensions. On one hand, it could mean obtaining talent, skills or information not present within the company. It could also be defined as reallocating the management and operation of a business activity to a different service provider. Some also define outsourcing as subcontracting non-revenue operations to consultants and professionals. Note that all the descriptions seem to involve a movement of services from one group to another, which is what outsourcing basically is.

There are different kinds of assistance and tasks that can be outsourced. Some of the more popular ones are Information Technology (IT) Outsourcing and Human Resource (HR) Outsourcing. Another kind would be Application Outsourcing. Each of these provides a number of advantages to the client organization; however, there can also be certain drawbacks.

Application Outsourcing

Application Management involves the support, preservation and development of existing services. When a company has activities that provide no revenue, or has problems with regards to productivity or the quality, predictability and responsiveness of a service, enterprises turn to Application Outsourcing. Application Outsourcing is actually one of the first types of outsourcing.

A number of issues may arise from this, though. An example will be who handles the documentation, the service provider or the client? What about the operation procedures? How should they be addressed? How should a company's processes be dealt with? Who will get the rights to the warranties?

Information Technology Outsourcing

Information Technology deals with the utilization of electronic devices for the processing of data. Its scope now involves, though it should already have been obvious, technology, and computing. Those involved in IT may have skills in data manipulation, networking, as well as in software designing.

Database and administration of systems are often included too. Information Technology Outsourcing is employed when a company has a lack in the ability to do IT functions. Also, IT is quite costly. Today, data is becoming more and more intricate and elaborate that handling it has become quite expensive. This is where outsourcing comes in. Outsourcing seems to be the solution for cheaper, yet quality service.

The issues for this kind of service have a wide scope. It could involve setbacks in software, equipment, and even people. A problem would certainly arise from lack in benchmarking, as well as when expected costs are not clearly defined, initially.

Human Resource Outsourcing

Human resources used to be exclusively synonymous to the word "labour", which is one of the four factors of production. The term has now evolved to mean something quite different to businesses and corporations. It now refers to the group of people or department who sees to the screening, hiring, training, firing personnel. In Human Resource Outsourcing, the agency examines, employs and then prepares workers for another enterprise.

Like the preceding services, a number of complications arise from such a setup. For example, the issue of whether the service provider will have allotted space within the company it lends its assistance to. The limits to what the department can do might also be unclear, and cultural differences may be present.

Outsourcing seems to be a very good and advantageous move for businesses, however, unless reviewed thoroughly, and terms set specifically, a number of problems may arise and what is supposed to make things lighter could do a 360 and become a burden.

Chapter 3: Models of Offshore Outsourcing

Offshore outsourcing is simply defined as outsourcing to outside countries. Some people may think that the process of offshore outsourcing is a walk in the park producing large sums of profits. This notion however is erroneous. It takes a lot of work and initiative to make offshore outsourcing work and produce desirable results. It involves choosing the right model of offshore outsourcing that would fit a particular business need or situation.

Choosing the right model of offshore outsourcing is a very critical phase that companies undergo. Any decision made can either make or break their business options offshore. Making the decision on what model to choose involves aspect of selecting which country, economic conditions of a country, international business strategy, and outsourcing strategy.

There are currently three models of offshore outsourcing that are popular among businesses. These three are outsourcing to a service provider, joint ventures and subsidiaries.

Outsourcing to a service provider

Outsourcing to a service provider is the most evident offshore outsourcing model. It has a lot of coverage that range from small projects to multi-year contracts that amount to millions of pounds.

The simplest form of outsourcing to a service provider is onsite subcontracting. In this form, a company assigns its skilled personnel directly at the client's site. The people assigned will then become part of the client's team. This form of offshore outsourcing is perhaps the simplest and is commonly used by small organizations that are tied with the client company.

Another form of outsourcing a service provider is pure offshore projects. In this form, the scope of the functions is properly defined and work can be done remotely that requires little to no supervision. A good example of this is assigning work to small organizations or even to individuals, freelancers as they are commonly called. With the help of online tools, projects can easily be sent and received by hired firms or individuals all over the world.

Offshore outsourcing individual projects is another form wherein a certain function is subdivided into smaller chunks to be outsourced to vendor companies. This is usually assigned to vendors with whom the company has close ties with.

Joint Venture Offshore Model

In this model of offshore outsourcing, one organization establishes a relationship with a local company wherein both companies contribute to their resources. The main purpose of this goal is "I lend you my strength and you lend me yours." This creates a win-win situation wherein both companies can gain something from the tie up. With this kind of setup, the client organization will be able to minimize the risks of offshore outsourcing while on the other hand the local firm is given the opportunity to work with a large company scaling up their value chain.

The joint venture offshore model is sometimes considered as the stepping stone of the client organization to move on to the next offshore outsourcing model which is the subsidiary offshore model.

Subsidiary Offshore Model

From the joint venture model, a company may transcend to the subsidiary offshore model. However, it is also possible for the client company to move directly with the subsidiary offshore model without passing through the joint venture model given that they have enough confidence and are comfortable with tackling the local market. The most challenging part in this kind of offshore outsourcing model is the general management of the onsite units especially the staff.

Conclusion

Offshore outsourcing is not as easy as some people may think it is. It needs thorough planning as well as making the right decisions. This includes choosing the right offshore outsourcing model that your company needs. It is even possible that a hybridization of the models is needed just to suit the needs of your organization. So plan well and choose well.

Chapter 4: Outsourcing: Why and How to Outsource your Business

Outsourcing is one of the latest buzzwords in the business world. It is an effective business solution that will truly benefit any company. Outsourcing means you will be hiring a third party company to do your company's business or at least part of it. So, why outsource your business when you can do the business of your company in-house?

The main reason why companies today are outsourcing their business or at least part of their business to other companies is that it is relatively cheaper than doing it in-house. For example, if your company needs a customer care department or a help desk, you will need a particularly large office space for this department and a lot of materials, such as computers, software and your company will also hire a large amount of manpower to act as call centre agents or help desk agents.

If you outsource it to call centre companies, you will definitely not need to hire additional employees and you will not need to purchase the technology needed to run an effective call centre department. You will also not need to devote an office space as the office can be in another country.

Companies prefer outsourcing in another country or offshore outsourcing, particularly in developing countries, such as India, Philippines, China, and countries in Latin America. This is because there is quite a large pool of talented individuals joining the workforce every year in these countries. Qualified and talented professionals in these countries can provide the same quality services as the qualified individuals in developed countries with companies that outsource their business or part of it, such as the United States, Canada, and countries in Europe.

This means that the companies who outsource their business in developing countries have access to cheap labour. They can save as much as half of their budget when they do not outsource or when they perform their businesses in-house.

Another reason is that the companies who outsource their business or part of their business will be able to focus more in the development of their company. Companies will be able to make full use of their facilities and resources for other important matters to make the company grow or improve.

The office space intended for the outsourced job can be used for another department. It can be an expansion of another department or it can be an entirely new department that the company may add.
Finding the right company to outsource your business can be rather easy to do. You actually don't have to travel to the country where you plan on outsourcing your business. All you have to do is search for it in your favourite search engine in the internet and you can expect a lot of results.

Since there are a lot of companies that offer outsourcing services, there will be a great chance that you will find a company that will suit your company's needs. It is recommended however that you should look for a company that is known to provide quality outsourced work. Find out if the company have ever worked with the same business you have in order to know that the company you plan on hiring have an experience in your field before.

Remember these things and you will know why outsourcing can definitely help your business and where and how to find the right company to get your business outsourced.

Chapter 5: Outsourcing: How it can Benefit your Business

The question of why businesses outsource their business process is still being asked by a lot of people. Surely, outsourcing would create a lot of profit for a business. Besides, why would businesses outsource their business process if they won't make any money out of it?

Aside from saving a lot of money from outsourcing, companies that want to unburden themselves from heavy workloads caused by the growing demand of their work by the public resort to outsourcing to do the job they should be doing. Businesses today hire outsourcing companies from different countries to do a part of the business process in order to save money on labour and also expand their capabilities.

Since there are a lot of skilled individuals in developing countries with little chance of employment, outsourcing became one of the best industries considered by a lot of talented and skilled individuals in developing countries. In terms of salary, outsourcing provides cheap labour compared to getting your companies work done in-house. For example, in the United States, you would pay a qualified professional about 100 dollars to get the job done. However, outsourcing the job to other countries will only require you to pay 20 dollars to get the same job done with an equally qualified professional and at the same time, keep them happy.

The minimum salary rate in developing countries is much lower compared in the United States or UK. This is why outsourcing can save your company a lot of money in terms of salary payments.

These are the benefits that your company can take advantage of in outsourcing. Cheap labour with equally qualified professionals in other countries can definitely save your company a lot of money on salaries.

However, before you try and outsource part of your company's work, you have to determine if the outsourcing company is the right company for you. Find out if the company is hiring qualified and are skilled professionals with skills related to your business. This will ensure the best quality for your outsourced jobs.

By first checking out the quality of work from an outsourcing company, you will be able to determine if the work done by them is up to par or not. If it is not, you can always go to other outsourcing companies and check out the quality of their work. Doing this will enable you to find the company that will meet your standards.

You also have to consider if the professionals who will be handling your outsourced work is qualified to do the job. Besides, you don't want a talented programmer to do the job of a mechanic. You have to know the specialty of the outsourcing company and determine if they will be able to perform the job you will offer them with quality and efficiency.

Outsourcing will answer your businesses financial and production problems. If you are looking for a way to save money and at the same time increase productivity, outsourcing is the right choice for your company. Not only will you save a lot of money because of cheaper labour compared as to the rates in your country, but you will also have the same quality of work that the equally qualified professionals in your country can do at a much lower price.

With outsourcing, your business will be able to grow and also decrease the burden of heavy workload.

Chapter 6: When Outsourcing is the Best Solution

There are times when outsourcing is the only option available for reasons such as no in-house employees are qualified or available to complete the particular task. However, there are also times when outsourcing is not the only option but it is also the best option. In these situations, outsourcing becomes a wise business decision as opposed to a requirement or a matter of personal preference. This book will discuss three situations where outsourcing is the best option. These options include:

1. When outsourcing saves money
2. When outsourcing helps make deadlines
3. When outsourcing increases productivity

When Outsourcing Saves Money

Outsourcing becomes the best solution when it saves the company money without compromising the quality of the work. Companies whose goals are predominately financial in nature often focus on the bottom line in determining whether or not to outsource projects or tasks. When the cost savings results in inferior work it is certainly not the best solution. However, companies who are able to outsource projects to highly qualified and capable individuals while still saving money enjoy the benefit of knowing they selected the best solution for their software related problems.

Whether or not outsourcing saves money is a concept which many have difficulty understanding. When most people think of outsourcing, they picture citizens of third world countries working for substandard wages but this is not an accurate representation of outsourcing. Nowadays outsourcing often involves hiring high priced, domestic consultants to tackle complex software problems under aggressive deadlines. This explanation makes the issue even more confusing for some who think it is impossible for it to be less expensive to hire a high priced consultant than to complete the task in-house.

Examining labour costs is often necessary to see how outsourcing can often reduce costs. Outsourcing may carry a higher per hour rate but it is important to note that the company is often not required to pay benefits such as social security, Medicare and workers" compensation to the consultant. Additionally, the consultant may work offsite meaning he is not putting a drain on company resources. Examining these factors is necessary to determine whether or not outsourcing is the best option.

When Outsourcing Helps Make Deadlines

Aggressive deadlines often make outsourcing the best available option. Most companies do not want to have to turn down work because they do not have enough staff members available to complete a particular project. Having the ability to outsource software jobs makes it easier for a company to compete for more jobs than their staff could possibly handle. This is because the managements know they have a network of consultants to rely on during times when schedules are tight. In these cases outsourcing becomes the best option.

Whether schedules are originally set to be rather aggressive or become accelerated due to problems earlier in the project they can become a hassle for many companies. Regardless of the cause of the scheduling concerns, clients may not understand if the consultant is unable to meet the required deadlines.

When Outsourcing Increases Productivity

Outsourcing also becomes the best solution to a problem when it results in increased productivity. Consider the tasks you intend to outsource and determine the amount of time it would take for these tasks to be completed in-house. Now consider the amount of time it would take to have these tasks completed through outsourcing. If the answer is outsourcing would be quicker, it is logical to go ahead and outsource these tasks. The reason for this is the consultant can be more efficient with the tasks.

When considering productivity it is also important to note that employees who are handling multiple tasks often take longer to complete each individual task then they would to complete each of these same tasks if they were his only responsibility. This is because employees who are multi-tasking are not necessarily as efficient as they believe they are. The main problem with multi-tasking is when switching from one activity there is a small delay each time the employee switches tasks because he often has to review his recent progress and remind himself what he intended to do next. Conversely outsourcing singular tasks allows the individual to focus 100% on each task.

Chapter 7: When Outsourcing is not a Good Idea

Outsourcing can really be beneficial for a number of reasons. Some companies enjoy benefits such as reduced labour costs, larger workforces, access to industry experts and increased flexibility through outsourcing. However, despite the obvious advantages to outsourcing there are some situations when outsourcing is not a good idea. Although there are number of scenarios where outsourcing is a viable business option there are other scenarios where outsourcing is not the best idea. In these situations it is best to keep the work in-house rather than attempting to make an outsourcing situation work out.

When Outsourcing is too Costly

One of the primary advantages of outsourcing is cost reduction. In many cases outsourcing results in reduced labour costs because costs such as social security, health care and workers" compensation are eliminated. Additionally, the increased efficiency resulting when tasks are outsourced to industry experts can also result in a cost reduction.

Despite these many opportunities for cost reductions, there are some situations where outsourcing might be the more expensive alternative and it may also lead to a financial loss instead of a gain. This may include a situation where the cost of outsourcing to a highly specialized expert exceeds the budget for the project. Fees for individuals with highly specialized degrees or areas of expertise are often quite expensive. Another possible situation is one where finding an individual qualified to complete specialized tasks would be too expensive of a process.

When Outsourcing Causes you to Lose Control

Even when tasks or projects are outsourced the company responsible for the work likes to continue to manage the project and keep close tabs on the progress of tasks. It is important for the company to continue to manage the project even after it has been outsourced because they are the ones who are ultimately responsible for the successful completion of the project. Whenever an individual or company wants to deny the company access to project files or documents, outsourcing is a bad idea. The company who has the vested interest in the outcome of the project should never be excluded from participating in making decisions regarding the project.

Before outsourcing a task or project care should be taken to establish criteria for the management of the project. Depending on the length and complexity of the project it may also be wise to schedule regular meetings to provide updates on the progress of the project. During this time the contractor should provide the employer with all documentation necessary to evaluate the progress of the project and verify it is still on track for completion by the established deadline.

When Outsourcing is not Permitted

Sometimes outsourcing is not a good idea simply because it is not permitted by contract requirements. Some project contracts may have stipulations stating the work cannot be outsourced to an individual or to another company. Inserting such a clause into a contract document is well within the rights of the clients. When they hire a particular company to complete a project or task, they expect all work related to the project or task to be completed by members of that company unless they specified otherwise when negotiating the contract. Violating the contract documents in this situation is not a good idea. The company could be penalized by the client. Penalties may include withholding payment or refusing to award future projects or tasks to the company.

Chapter 8: Offshore Outsourcing: Finding the Right Country to Outsource your Company's Projects

Today, companies are now hiring other companies in other countries to do their business or part of their business. This particular type of business strategy is called offshore outsourcing.

It is a fact that in today's business world, offshore outsourcing is now becoming a very feasible trend for companies who wants to expand their business or to simply reduce their overhead expenses.

As an entrepreneur, you would definitely want to reduce the operating costs of your business without sacrificing your businesses functionality. By outsourcing your business or at least part of your business, you can indeed expand and reduce operating expenses. Outsourcing is a very large industry in developing countries, such as India and the Philippines. Your company can definitely hire companies in these two countries to outsource part of your business or even all of it. However, you should take note that you should choose an outsourcing company that provides quality and professionally done jobs.

You should also consider which country you should outsource your business in. People in different countries have different culture and education. You have to choose which people, culture, and educational standards that your company can benefit from.

For example, in India, this country has one of the largest populations of IT professionals in the world. Because of the British influenced educational systems in this country, the education on math and science in this country is greatly emphasized. This country has more than one hundred and twenty thousand trained IT professionals added to the workforce every year.

India is now being considered as an IT centre in developing countries and is also one of the countries that United States and UK companies prefer for software or IT outsourcing. India has created a strong reputation as one of the leading countries in IT outsourcing industry in the world.

In the Philippines, it is an entirely different story. Because this nation is considered as Asia's English speaking countries that have 94% literacy rate, this country is also considered to have a large population of IT professionals in the world. With over three million University graduates joining the workforce every year, this country is indeed one of the best source for talent.

Although the Filipinos are Asian, it was influenced by Americans for over 50 years and has developed a western culture. Filipinos loves watching American television and because of this, the people in the Philippines are fluent in American English and can communicate effectively with Americans and other English speaking nations.

Because the Filipinos are fluent in American English, this country have become a premier choice of the United States for call centre outsourcing. If you are looking for call centre services that are able to provide quality customer support service, the Philippines is definitely the country to look for call centres. Although India charges less for its call centre services than in the Philippines, more companies in the United States prefer the Philippines more for customer care jobs because of the quality of work they offer.

Another factor that the Philippines is chosen for call centre jobs is that not only that the people speak fluent American English, but they are also friendly and helpful in nature.

These are the things you should consider when choosing a country to outsource your business or at least part of your business. You also have to consider the people living in it and the culture they were brought up with in order to know where to outsource your company's project.

40

Chapter 9: Try Outsourcing when you Need an eBook Written

Writing eBooks is one activity which is outsourced with a great deal of frequency. EBooks are books which are published and distributed in a software format. Some consider them to be much more convenient than regular books because they can be downloaded to computers, laptops and a number of multimedia devices making it convenient for the individual to take the eBook with them everywhere they go. Another advantage of eBooks is they are typically less expensive than traditional books. This is because the publishing costs associated with publishing an eBooks is significantly lower than it is for publishing regular books. Outsourcing the writing of eBooks is a fairly common practice. There are a few simple guidelines which should be followed when selecting the perfect writer for the job and outsourcing the project.

Select an Accomplished Writer

One of the most basic guidelines for outsourcing an eBook is to select an accomplished writer who has experience relative to your niche subject. While giving a chance to a new writer is certainly noble, an eBook is not the ideal situation for making such a noble gesture. If you feel strongly about a particular writer who does not have relevant experience try offering him the opportunity to complete a smaller job for you such as a website article. An eBook is a large project in which you invest a great deal of time, money and energy and you want to be sure the end results are of a high quality.

Assist in the Creation of the Book Outline

The outline for an eBook is very important and should be established before work on the eBook commences. It is acceptable to make minor changes to the outline during the course of the project but the bulk of the outline should remain the same. This is important because a well developed outline will assist in creating a logical flow to the material presented in the eBook.

The client should always take an active role in developing the outline for the eBook. The writer may have ideas about the content he wants to include or believes is relevant but the responsibility for making the decision regarding what belongs in the eBooks is ultimately up to the client. Establishing an outline ahead of time will ensure there are no surprises when the final work is submitted.

Have the eBook Edited Independently

The final tip we have to offer for outsourcing an eBook is to have the eBook edited independently rather than allowing the writer to edit the eBook. The writer may do an excellent job creating high quality content that is accurate, informative and interesting and may also do a fairly good job of proofreading the document but it is always worthwhile to have a fresh pair of eyes review the document. They are not as familiar with the project so they are more likely to notice errors which were previously overlooked by the writer who may miss the errors because when he was proofreading he knew what he meant to write and subconsciously makes the correction as he is reading through the document.

The other advantage of having the eBook edited independently is that the editor can review the document in reference to the outline to ensure all of the necessary subjects were adequately covered in the eBook.

If you need help on this, please feel free to contact me via this link.
http://www.bpo.aaglobalsourcing.com/contact-bpo

Chapter 10: Top Writers Around the World Will Write for you – Outsourcing

The content of your site tells a whole lot about your website. They will basically describe what your site is about and also tell people what your site has to offer. Articles and website content makes a whole lot of difference in your site because they can catch the attention of your website visitors and keep them in there.

With good website content you get the benefit of clearly depicting what it is you want to share with people. Also, good content and articles can lead people to your site. With more traffic, you get to earn more from your site making it profitable. A sites success, be it for profit or not, is the number of the flow of traffic in your site.

So how does good content and great articles get you traffic? Well, many search engines rely on the keyword and keyword phrases of a site to put it in their results list. If your content contains a good number of keywords and keywords phrases, it may be chosen to be a part of the top listed sites in the search result pages.

But before you think of just plastering your site with all the keywords and keyword phrases it could hold, search engines also filter out that abuse. You must have good well written articles that incorporate the keywords and keyword phrases properly in their content and articles.

There are many of those who cannot afford the time to write their own website contents and articles. While writing content and articles specifically designed for the internet may take some getting used to and some researching and learning, there are many writers that can be found all over the world who could do it for you.

Many of us do not have the time to learn web content writing and article writing designed for the internet. There are writers who have great experience in doing this and charge only a minimal fee for such work. Writers like this can be regarded as experts in this style of writing and can greatly help your website to get that coveted spot in the search engine rankings.

Other than getting your site in the web results page of search engines, they can also provide your site with meaningful articles and content that can impress your website visitors and entice others to view your site. Every website could use the extra traffic website visitors could invite.

Then there are those who need papers to be done either for their school or office work. Top writers around the world are very knowledgeable and do extreme researching to get a job done right. They are also very adept in many writing styles that are needed to best suit the client's need.

Many writers around the world charge a minimal fee depending on the type of writing job needed and the number of words needed in the content. Usually, a two hundred fifty worded article would cost from 4 to 8 dollars depending on the writers experience and ability. This is a small price to pay for having a content rich site or for a well researched and written paper.

There are also many sites that can offer you these services with their team of well trained and experienced writers. They offer many writing services to cover any writing needs. A writer can be based anywhere in the world and are guaranteed to offer good contents and articles. Each one are doubly checked, edited and proofread so that you would get your money's worth.

Finding a good writer or a site that offers these kinds of services is simply done by searching for them in search engines. Type down your keyword or keyword phrase (e.g. Content Writers, Article Writers) and you will see a long list of sites that offer these services.

The top sites would probably be the best since they have done a good job of keeping their content at a high quality to get them high rankings. But you may also want to shop around and read some of their sample work to get an idea of how much it will cost you.

If you need help on this, please feel free to contact me via this link.
http://www.bpo.aaglobalsourcing.com/contact-bpo

Chapter 11: Tips for Outsourcing eBooks

EBooks are quickly becoming very popular in the Internet niche marketing industry. EBooks are essentially books which are available in software formats and distributed either through email or Internet downloads. There is usually a fee associated with downloading an eBook. These fees are usually considerably lower than the fees associated with purchasing a hardcopy of a similar book. This is because eBooks are typically less expensive to publish. With so many Internet niche marketers relying on eBooks as part of their marketing campaigns, it is certainly understandable that many are beginning to outsource the writing of eBooks to professional writers. As eBooks become more popular and the level of competition rises, it is necessary for the quality of the eBooks to increase as well making it essential to outsource these projects to qualified candidates. However, many may have concerns about the process of outsourcing. This book addresses these concerns by providing tips for outsourcing eBooks with success.

Select the Right Person for the Job

The first step in outsourcing an eBook with a great deal of success is taking the screening process seriously and finding the most qualified candidate to write the eBook. When searching for a candidate to write an eBook, place a detailed advertisement specifying the exact project requirements including subject, length, milestone goals and ultimate deadline. This is important because it ensures candidates are aware of all of the requirements before they apply.

You may still receive countless applications from those who are unqualified but that is where carefully screening the applicants becomes imperative. In reviewing applications pay particular attention to the quality of samples provided, the amount of relevant work completed and the ability of the candidate to following the instructions in the advertisement. All of these elements will make simplify the screening process by enabling you to eliminate those who do not follow instructions or provide quality samples of relevance to the project.

Next narrow the list of candidates to a few who are most qualified and interview these candidates further. EBooks can most often be written by candidates from remote locations so there is usually not a need for in person interviews especially if there is a geographical distance between the candidate and the buyer. Phone interviews and online interviews are sufficient substitutes. After the interviews determine which, if any, of the candidates is most qualified and offer the opportunity to complete the project to this candidate. If none of the candidates seem just right it might be necessary to continue looking and screening new candidates.

Be Involved in Developing the Outline

Once a professional writer is accepted for a particular project, it is time to start developing an outline for the project, if this has not already been done. The marketer should be heavily involved in doing this so they can ensure the eBook includes all of the information they believe is necessary. Asking the writer to contribute ideas to the outline is appropriate but it is accepted that the client will provide the majority of these details rather than relying on the writer to do so.

Maintain Final Editing Rights

Finally the client should always maintain final editing rights in any eBook they commission. They may work closely with the writer during the process of writing the book but upon completion the eBook should be reviewed and edited carefully. This process should include editing the eBook for grammar and sentence structure, flow and style, accuracy of content and any other elements deemed of importance by the client. The client is the one ultimately responsible for the information contained in the eBook and he should do his best to ensure the eBook he provides is not only interesting and informative but also accurate. This is especially important in situations where medical issues are discussed.

Another important reason to maintain finally editing rights is to ensure all stipulations by advertisers are met accordingly. Many eBooks are sponsored by individuals or companies who expect their website, products or services to be recommended in the eBook in exchange for their sponsorship. For this reason care should be taken to review the final version of the eBook to ensure the sponsor's needs are met and that direct competitors are not touted as being superior to the sponsor.

If you need help on this, please feel free to contact me via this link.
http://www.bpo.aaglobalsourcing.com/contact-bpo

Chapter 12: How Outsourcing Book Keeping can Help your Business

As a business owner, you know that you have to record every financial aspect in your business. It is required by law. The books you record it into will be for tax purposes and the figures should be accurate. However, you have to consider the fact that if you own a business, there will be too much things in your mind and you will often tend to forget about doing the books. Being negligent on this part can incur serious penalties. If you don't have enough time for book keeping, then you might want to try outsourcing book keeping for your business.

Today, many companies are now outsourcing book keeping jobs in order to save time and be more efficient in running their business. Besides, if you let other people do your books, then you will be able to concentrate more on running your business. Outsourcing book keeping is also very popular as it is very cheap.

You have to consider that outsourcing has become a trend in today's business world. Because it is a lot cheaper to outsource than to have an in house book keeper or accountant, many businesses today are now outsourcing their book keeping jobs.

These are the advantages of outsourcing book keeping. It will not only give you more time to concentrate in running your business, but it will also save you a lot of money.

However, before you hire a book keeper to do this kind of job for you, you first need to remember that you have to choose the right book keeping service first.

The first thing that you need to look for is the qualifications of the book keeping services company. The staff should be knowledgeable in the field of book keeping, and they should also be certified professional book keepers.

Besides the qualification, they also need to be experienced in the field of book keeping and are knowledgeable in the inner workings of businesses especially about financial transactions in businesses. You have to remember that one doesn't need to hold a degree as an accountant in order to become a good book keeper. Normally, everyone can become a book keeper. The most important thing that you should look for in a book keeper is experience.

The portfolio of the book keeping services company you look for should also be good. The more clients they have, it will mean that they are trusted by people. Besides, as a businessman, you too would understand the fact that people will only buy the services of businesses that they trust.

These are the things that you should look for in book keeping services companies when you plan on outsourcing your book keeping jobs to them. By having all the mentioned traits, you can be sure that you will be able to get your books back in time for tax time.

Remember these tips and you will be able to have more time on running your business and save a lot of money.

By outsourcing book keeping for your online business, you can be sure that you will have nothing to worry about when tax time comes. Just remember that you have to give the book keeper you hire all the necessary information about your business and also your financial records.

Chapter 13: Offering Outsourcing Bookkeeping Services Must be Perfect to be Successful

In a changing world, with globalization, technological advances and a continual revalidation of methods of doing business, business owners have choices when it comes to managing time and business. Business needs to maintain their financial and accounting record as this helps it in the long run. The business is workings then it means that the financial and accounting status of the firm is properly managed. A detailed representation of the business accounting functions is conscientiously done by the professional accountants of the outsourcing firm. Hence it is understood that any business will be spending a significant resource in hiring and maintaining this division.

Bookkeeping is an essential business tool for any size of company to help them record all the financial transaction. Bookkeeping could be server based.

If the client does require that his accounts books be maintained in his own computer, the outsourcing bookkeeping connects to the client's computer through the internet. This is done with the use of remote desktop access services.

Outsourcing Business without e-communication is it possible! Here Outsourcing bookkeeping Services has try to explain something about e-accounting services.

Bookkeeping outsourcing handled by a seller in other country would help the business in saving a significant amount in terms of human and financial source.

Some of these methods are data entry bookkeeping, single entry bookkeeping, commercial bookkeeping, one-write systems, computerized systems the most commonly used method of bookkeeping.

Normal bookkeeping with details concerning transactions, turn over, and profit and loss generations helps business owners a great deal in getting loans from different public and private financial sources. Accounting data entry, payroll preparation, cash flow, bank and credit card reconciliation, trial balance, accounts payable management and other bookkeeping tasks which need updates every month can be reorganized and restructured in few very easy steps.

There are two types of Bookkeeping Services: on-site arrangement and off-site arrangement. Bookkeeping outsourcing is therefore a big help for financial institutions by not only making properly maintained and processed accounting data available at a short notice, but also enabling the business to employ the resources, thus made available, in other divisions as well.

Bookkeeping can be done manually or can be computerized, depending on the size of the business and transaction volumes. Bookkeeping Service providers" solutions are modified to meet business requirements. A powerful combination of technology, people and processes can boost the business. Then the task of handling sensitive financial data and maintaining accounts can safely be handed over to a bookkeeping outsourcing firm. Outsource your bookkeeping today; and focus on those functions of their businesses that really matters for its growth.

Chapter 14: Choosing your Outsourcing Bookkeeping Partner

Outsourcing can be defined as the process of assigning business processes to a 3rd party service provider. The outsourcing industry came to reputation as part of a business during the 1980s when several European airline companies started to transfer part of their back office function to New Delhi. This move resulted from the companies having to lower the costs of labour.

However today, outsourcing has a driving force far greater than just cutting down costs – of course it still part of the many reasons for outsourcing but the list of the benefits it provides has grown. And as companies around the world starting to realize this, the number of people and organizations providing outsourcing services has also boomed. This growth consequently requires companies to do better in choosing their partners when outsourcing. This principle applies when choosing an outsourcing vendor providing bookkeeping services.

The very important aspect when choosing is to identify the right outsourcing partner that will fit to your preferences as well as your bookkeeping needs. Practices and guidelines that the service provider follows impact your businesses directly. This is the reason why your potential partners should undergo the eyes of scrutiny to be able to choose the right one for you and your business. Be patient – do not rush.

Guidelines when Choosing your Outsourcing Partner

Here are a few guidelines you may want to follow when choosing your outsourcing partner.

1. Experience is one of the greatest factors that make a company grow. This is the reason why if you want competitive companies to handle your bookkeeping functions, choose someone that possess the skills as well as the experience in this field. You can have an overview of the organizations total client base and the different kinds of project they have handled. Information such as the two will give you an idea of their standing in the outsourcing market. It is a good habit to check on the references the company provides you.

2. Do a background check running the organization you want to partner up with. Get the profile of the head person as well as the profiles of other key personnel. You should also take into consideration their credentials and qualifications to know whether the people that will possibly handle your bookkeeping functions are competitive enough to do the job.

3. Feedbacks of other clients are always added information you can take into consideration when choosing your future partner. Check if the service providers indeed can meet the expectations of their clients. This is one way

of gauging their ability in the field of customer service.

4. It will not be too much to ask to give them some kind of exam or test. Give files that already have been completed. You can then evaluate their skills in bookkeeping with the output they provide by comparing it previous work.

5. Compile all the information you have gathered and do your assessment. You should also not disregard your gut feeling. Even if they gather good results, if you do not feel comfortable working with the organization, then as much as possible, look for other service providers.

You should remember that even though bookkeeping is non-core business function, it is still very important for the company as whole. Thus, it is very important that you choose the right group of people to handle this delicate task so as to avoid complications in the future.

Chapter 15: Outsourcing your Marketing Needs

Have you ever stopped to notice that your marketing campaigns and activities are not paying off, or getting your desired result? So, you are spending a fortune on marketing booths, exhibits, brochures, flyers and so on and still your client database has not improved? Have you ever stopped to think what are you doing wrong? What is it that you lack?

You may have a pool of right-brain creative people in your marketing team, producing impressive brochures and coming up with great exhibit ideas, but do they have the left-brain analytical people for a better understanding of the statistics and trends in the modern-day information and tech-savvy market? I guess not.

This is the usual reason why most companies waste time, money and effort on futile marketing campaigns and activities-they do not have the right people for understanding the market.

Yes, they have the creative ones but that is not enough to generate the result your company is aiming for. These creative people of yours may only be wasting their creative talent because it is not well-aimed at the target. Fortunately, more and more companies are realizing this mistake and so they are now outsourcing their marketing needs for a more focused and successful marketing endeavours.

The trend started with outsourcing only a part of the marketing function, which is the advertising. Now, companies are already outsourcing the more nitty-gritty marketing tasks such as customer analytics, lead management and direct-mail management. What used to be simple marketing tasks have now been realized as very significant factors that can greatly help boost marketing success.

Marketing outsourcing business companies have recognized this importance and have focused on producing experts in these fields so they could provide the best service to their clients. So, these days, services for these seemingly mundane but very important marketing tasks, can be outsourced for better results.

And a lot of companies are realizing the sense in the idea. A recent survey reported that 53% of polled marketing executives are now planning to outsource their marketing needs. They now realize that outsourcing marketing activities saves the company marketing cost, while at the same time producing improved quality work that generates the result they wanted.

Also, they see now that mass marketing is no longer reliable for reaching more prospective customers because nowadays, communication has become more complicated than ever, hence, it needs expertise on computer aided analysis. And this is what marketing outsourcing business companies have and offer.

However, this does not mean that marketing executives and officers of the company are no longer needed. The opposite is true.

While the activities are outsourced, there is a vital role for the marketing executive to play-they still need to build and maintain good working relationships with their clients and customers.

The good working relationship still rests with them because customers still need to see the company in flesh and blood, despite the convenience of outsourced computerized services on the Internet. The marketing executives, of course, still have to oversee the production and progress of the marketing activities that are being outsourced.

Of course, that still has to be managed and monitored to ensure the company get the best result. Also, they are to build good working relationship with these outside suppliers to ensure that the company's specific needs are met. As in every business, success lies in building and maintaining good working relationships with both the clients and the suppliers.

Chapter 16: Software Outsourcing: a Cheap Way to Run your Business

Outsourcing is now one of the most popular terms you will hear in the business world. Obviously, it is something that companies benefit from because companies today are extensively using outsourcing as part of their company. Since companies benefit from outsourcing, you would want to consider outsourcing to also be part of your company.

However, you first have to know what outsourcing is in order to fully understand how it can help your company and why this service is so in demand in the business world today.

You may wonder why companies outsource their business process when you can do it the old way and take care of your business process in-house. The reason for this is that companies will save a lot of money when they outsource their business process in other countries in companies that accepts outsourced jobs.

This is because companies that accept outsourcing jobs from other countries already have the facilities and the manpower to do the business process that your company will give them. This means that you will not purchase the necessary facilities and hire the necessary manpower in order to get the job done properly Also, these offshore companies that accepts outsourcing jobs will charge cheaper rates to get it done and they also hire talented professionals who are qualified to get the job done for you.

Another reason why outsourcing is preferred by more companies today is that they can focus more on important matters concerning the company. By outsourcing a part of your business process, your company will be able to fully use all the resources it needs in order for your company to stay competitive.
For example, if your company makes software, you will need a help desk in order to interact with your clients and to answer any problems that your clients may have. If you don't outsource your help desk, you will need to make use of additional workspace, purchase the necessary technology to start an effective help desk, such as computers and help desk software, and you will also need to hire help desk representatives with full company benefits to man the workstations.

By outsourcing your help desk to call centers located in other countries, you will be able to save a lot of office space to be used for more important company functions. Also, you will be able to save a lot of money from purchasing the technology and hiring full time employees and your company can concentrate more on vital factors.

Today, more and more software development companies are now considering outsourcing their software development program to IT companies in developing countries, such as India, China, and the Philippines. These countries are known to be full of talented IT professionals who are able to develop the software you need in order to satisfy your clients. And, they also charge half of the fee that an IT professional in your country may charge you.

These are the benefits that outsourcing will give your software company. By outsourcing your software development program, such as .Net, Java programming, and other business solution software, you will be able to save a lot of money for your company and at the same time, let your company focus more on important matters to keep your company competitive in today's business world.

Chapter 17: Is Outsourcing the Answer to your Software Problems?

Determining whether or not outsourcing is the answer to your software problems is not necessarily a difficult question but it is a question which involves careful consideration. There are a series of questions which should be asked to help determine whether or not outsourcing is a wise decision in a particular case. Examples of some of the questions which should be asked are:

1. Are there in-house employees capable or resolving the software problem?
2. Do current workloads allow in-house employees to work on this problem?
3. How expensive will it be to outsource the task?
4. What are the benefits of outsourcing the problem?

This book will take a look at each of these questions and provide insight into how these questions can be used to help make this important decision.

The Capabilities of In-house Employees

Some software problems require highly specialized training to resolve the issues. It is often the case that a company's in-house employees do not have the capabilities of resolving these software issues. When this occurs outsourcing the problem to a specialist is the obvious choice. However, in situations where the in-house employees are qualified to resolve the problem, the issue of whether or not to outsource becomes more complicated.

Those tasked with making the decision often weight the options by considering the cost of outsourcing versus the speed at which the problem would be resolved in both cases. If there is an expert readily available to tackle the problem it will likely be resolved relatively quickly. However, if in-house employees are currently overburdened, they may not be able to make this problem a priority.

The Workload of In-house Employees

The workload of in-house employees often comes into question when considering whether or not to outsource specific software related task or tasks. In the previous section we discussed the importance of outsourcing when the in-house employees are not qualified for certain tasks. However, this is not always the case. Often in-house employees are fully capable of completing a task but they are unable to do so because of their current workload. In a situation when all of the in-house employees are unavailable to take on additional tasks, outsourcing again becomes a viable option.

Will Outsourcing Save Money

One of the main factors company's consider when they contemplate outsourcing is whether or not they will save money by outsourcing. Hiring an expert on a contract basis can certainly be expensive but it is often a worthwhile investment especially for highly specialized work. The cost of outsourcing is usually higher in terms of the hourly rate of the employee but overall the costs may be reduced. When considering work performed by in-house employees it is important to realize the cost of the work includes the employee's hourly rate, the cost of benefits such as social security, Medicare and workers" compensation and resources such as office space, hardware, office supplies and other incidentals. After factoring in all of these costs it becomes clear that outsourcing is not always the more expensive option.

Another factor to consider when calculating the costs of outsourcing a software problem is how quickly the problem can be resolved by outsourcing as opposed to handling the problem in-house. This will depend on the capabilities and availability of the in-house staff. If there is not a capable staff member available it may take significantly longer to handle the problem in-house.

The Benefits of Outsourcing

Finally, the benefits of outsourcing should be considered in deciding whether or not to outsource particular tasks. We have already touched upon some of the benefits of outsourcing but for the sake of completeness we will include a list of some of the most significant benefits below:

1. Decreased labour costs
2. Access to industry experts
3. Flexibility in scheduling
4. Increased manpower

With so many benefits it is clear that outsourcing can be a viable solution to many software problems. The bottom line in determining whether or not to outsource a particular software problem often involves comparing the benefits of outsourcing to the costs of outsourcing.

Chapter 18: IT Outsourcing Industry: Why it is so Hot

Nowadays, you will hear outsourcing a lot of times in the business world. Why? This is because outsourcing can provide quality jobs for companies at a very fast rate and at a very cheap price. This is the reason why many companies in the United States, Canada, and as well as in European countries are now considering to outsource some of their IT jobs.

Outsourcing is a very large industry in developing countries, such as India, Philippines, and China. Outsourcing creates jobs for these countries for their talented and qualified IT professionals.

Today, software companies are required to produce a lot of different kinds of software product for their clients. The products they produce are usually for large organizations, such as financial institutions, large corporate houses, and government bodies. The software IT companies produce are used by these companies or organizations for their everyday work and for business solutions.

However, with more and more demand for these kinds of software, you have to realize that it will require IT software companies a lot of investment capital in infrastructure and as well as large manpower to work on these software.

The IT industry is a very competitive industry where you want your IT Company to be the best in the industry and the number one producer of software for large organizations and companies. But because of the huge amount of investment you need to build your company and also because of the increasing numbers of IT companies worldwide, it will be difficult for your company to grow.

However, there is one way you can let your company be one of the best in the industry and allow it to grow at a very low price. Today, outsourcing is one of the best business solutions in your IT company. You will now be able to save a lot of money if you consider outsourcing. Developing countries, such as China, Philippines, and India have a lot of qualified IT professionals working in an outsourcing company. You can hire a particular IT outsourcing company in these developing countries in order to let your company grow.

First of all, outsourcing your IT jobs will enable you to save a lot of money on infrastructure and manpower because the outsourcing company will be able to provide both. They have talented and skilled IT professionals qualified to do your company's job. Secondly, outsourcing can also let your company's resources focus more on the company's development and growth. You will be able to set aside these jobs to outsourcing companies and concentrate on more important factors in your company. And lastly, you will be getting quality work as outsourcing companies in these developing countries have the required skills to do the job.

Most of the jobs that IT companies in Europe, Unites States, and Canada outsource are creating software in .Net, database solutions, Java/J2EE, smartcard solution and also in wireless application developments. Help desk, and call centres are also one of the most popular jobs outsourced by large companies in the United States.

In order to get the best company to outsource your company's project, you have to consider that the company you will hire should be able to provide good quality work in order to get your money's worth. The country that the company is in should also have favourable government policies and should be willing to invest in the IT and outsourcing industry.

This is why outsourcing is one of the hottest trends in businesses today.

Chapter 19: Precautions for Outsourcing Software Jobs

Outsourcing software jobs is certainly a viable business solution for all types of industries. Software plays an integral part in many different industries and because software is constantly evolving and developing it isn't always feasible to employ an in-house software staff capable of meeting complex software needs. Companies may find the ability to outsource software projects while still maintaining a certain degree of profitability; however, there are a few caveats to doing this.

Outsourcing software jobs is a sound business practice but care should be taking to avoid certain pitfalls often associated with outsourcing work. Taking a few precautions can prevent the company from making mistakes while outsourcing such as outsourcing the work to individuals or companies who lack necessary qualifications, making fatal scheduling errors and spending too much money to outsource the project.

Properly Screening Outsourcing Candidates

One of the most common mistakes made in outsourcing software projects is delegating the project to an individual who lacks the necessary qualifications and capabilities to complete the project efficiently. Companies who regularly outsource work may establish working relationships with individuals they are confident will perform well but before these types of relationships are established it will be necessary to carefully screen each potential candidate before outsourcing a job.

There are precautions companies can take when they are considering outsourcing a software project to ensure the candidate they select is well qualified to complete the project. The following are a few of the basic precautions companies should take:

1. Describe the project sufficiently in job advertisements.
2. Review applications and resumes carefully.
3. Schedule interviews with qualified candidates.
4. Ask interview candidates to provide a list of work references.
5. Verify each reference and check the validity of work history.

Establishing Schedules when Outsourcing

Another mistake often made by companies who outsource is to fail to establish a firm schedule. This may not be especially harmful when the schedule of the project is flexible but it can be a serious mistake when the schedule of the project is not flexible.

Finding a candidate who is qualified to handle outsourcing work is important but it is also important to find a candidate who is available when you need someone to complete the work. This is a significant point because some candidates may be well qualified but if they are not available when you need them they are not an ideal candidate to complete the project.

It is best to discuss scheduling upfront when screening outsourcing candidates. This is important because it can be costly to spend time finding a candidate only to find out they are unavailable towards the end of the screening process.

Spending Too Much Money on Outsourcing

One final mistake companies often make when outsourcing is spending too much money on outsourcing. This includes money paid to the individual or firm to complete the work as well as money invested in finding the most qualified candidate.

One precaution to take when considering outsourcing is to investigate all of the costs associated with outsourcing and establish a budge for having a particular project completed as an outsourcing endeavour before beginning to search for potential candidates. Doing this will enable companies to evaluate whether or not outsourcing is a wise decision from a financial standpoint before they invest too much in the process.

When evaluating the costs associated with outsourcing a software project it is important to consider a number of factors. First evaluate the amount the client is paying for the completion of the project. Next assess the in-house effort which will be required for this project including management and recruiting candidates to complete the project. Determine the percentage of the budget which will be consumed by these efforts. Now it is time to look at the remaining budget and determine how much can be invested in outsourcing the project while still remaining profitable. The fees paid to the independent contractor or consulting firm should not be so high that they do not enable the company to profit from the project.

Chapter 20: Internet Marketing and Outsourcing

Internet marketing and outsourcing work very well together. In fact most Internet marketers employ at lease some degree of outsourcing.

The most common aspects of Internet marketing which are outsourced are copywriting and website design. Ideally these tasks will be delegated to individuals who are skilled in search engine optimization (SEO). Additionally, those who manage multiple niches may opt to outsource the responsibilities of managing some of their niche markets. This article will take a look at some of the commonly outsourced tasks and provide information regarding why outsourcing these tasks is ideal.

Managing Multiple Niches

Many involved in Internet niche marketing become involved in managing multiple niche marketing campaigns. When this happens it can become difficult for one individual to oversee all of the campaigns without compromising the quality of the niche markets. Therefore, he will often outsource the oversight responsibilities related to managing some of the niche markets. This gives him the freedom to focus more on developing new niches and marketing strategies as opposed to overseeing minute details.

Care should be taken when outsourcing this type of work to ensure the employee hired to undertake these tasks is an honest individual with a great deal of integrity. Those who are lacking in integrity may take advantage of this situation to learn about the marketing strategies for the express purpose of stealing sensitive information and creating competition in these niches.

Outsourcing Copywriting

Copywriting services are also commonly outsourced in niche marketing. Those involved in Internet niche marketing realize the importance of providing high quality content that is also optimized for search engines. This applies to copywriting which is included on niche websites, in e-newsletters, in press releases and in ebooks. The content provided is critical to the success of the niche marketing campaign because it is often the first impression members of the target audience get of the campaign. Their opinion of the copy can determine whether or not they are willing to visit the niche website in the future or further research products or services for sale.

When selecting a writer to provide the content for the niche marketing campaign, it is important to consider a writer with SEO experience. This is important because the content provided on websites can have an impact on the search engine rankings of the website. The use of keywords is the most important part of copywriting relevant to SEO. The keywords should be used in a manner that creates informative and interesting copy that appeals to both website visitors and search engines.

Outsourcing Website Design

Web design is another aspect of Internet niche marketing that is often outsourced. Most marketers recognize website design as an important part of their success. They need their websites to be well designed both aesthetically and technically to ensure visitors enjoy the website and all of the features of the website operate smoothly.

Additionally, it is very important for the website designer chosen to understand how to implement SEO strategies into the design of the website. There are many different strategies available for SEO and there are also always new techniques being developed, tested and evaluated. The SEO of a website is pretty much a full time job. This is why it is essential for marketers to outsource this work so they can ensure they have someone working on their website optimization constantly.

Chapter 21: All About Hospitalists and why Companies are Outsourcing Them

Firstly, you have to understand what a hospitalist is. Hospitalists are doctors who specialize or focus on hospital medicine. Meaning these doctors consider the hospital as their office. Hospitalists are involved in patient care, research, teaching and leadership related to hospital care.

Hospitalists focus around the site of care, which is the hospital, unlike cardiology, that focuses on a single organ and oncology that focuses on diseases. Hospitalists help manage patient care in the hospital. They often see patients in the ER, admit them to inpatient wards, and cares for them even after being hospitalized.

The activity of a hospitalist focuses on hospital care for inpatients. They provide another way to improve and also assist in the traditional patient-doctor relationship. They also do not have any outside practices and focuses. Because of this, hospitalists are able to take care and have more time for hospital patients.

Today, there are organizations and companies that provide hospitalist physicians in hospitals all over the world in a contractual basis. This is because they are able to provide service to primary healthcare physicians who are regulars in the hospital's medical staff. This means that they will be responsible for outpatient and emergency room care patients if a member of the medical staff doesn't want the responsibility.

Another benefit that the hospital can take advantage of if they hire Hospitalists is that they will be able to move patients to the recovery process faster. Hospitals will now be able to do this without sacrificing the quality of hospital care. This means that it will eventually ease the frequent needs of the hospital on holding patients in the emergency department and also on the admission.

Hospitalist programs can eventually benefit the physicians, the hospital and the patient:

For physicians, it will enable regular healthcare physicians to concentrate in their medical practice. This will also allow them to improve their skills and it will also enable them to use their time more efficiently. The hospitalist system will eventually eliminate or at least decrease the on-call responsibility of primary healthcare physicians on patients who are not yet assigned to a physician, and it will also have reimbursement advantages.

Hospitals will also benefit from hospitalist programs. This is because it actually reduces the patient's length of stay and the hospital costs to about 15%. This program will also decrease the number of admissions that are inappropriate and the number of days denied for managed care companies. A hospitalist program also provides satisfaction rating for the patient and the family and it also improves relationship between the physician and the patient.

For patients, studies have found that after being taken care of hospitalists, patients also prefers the hospitalist concept rather than wanting their own doctor to take care of them during their stay at the hospital. The hospitalist is always in the hospital and is readily available for the patient's needs. They will be able to answer questions from both the families and the patients.

Think of hospitalists as outsourced physicians by a company. Hospitals now hire outsourced hospitalists in order to improve the quality of hospital care and to satisfy their in-house medical staff and also their patient. Having hospitalists in a hospital will ensure round-the-clock quality care for patient and at the same time, reduce the cost that a hospital may spend for patients.

They will be the ones who will admit, and take care of the patient on the duration of time they are admitted in the hospital. With hospitalists, you will never again wait for your doctor to take care of you. Care will always be there 24 hours a day and 7 days a week.

Chapter 22: Medical Transcription Outsourcing

Outsourcing has been practiced by different companies for quite some time now. A lot of people in the business world have seen the advantages it brings to companies. In fact, even medical transcriptions are now being outsourced either to local or foreign companies specializing in medical transcription. This is what is called medical transcription outsourcing.

What is Medical Transcription?

Medical Transcription, also known by the abbreviation MT, is a process wherein recorded dictations by health care professionals or physician about a patient's medical record are converted or transcribed into written text.

Of course, transcribing is not simply typing. It has its own set of rules and follows establish and prescribed document formats. This is also the reason why Medical Transcriptionists should be skilled and trained in the medical field. This includes being able to distinguish and spell out correctly different medical terms.

Most of today's medical transcription companies make use of specialized computers to be able to provide the best possible results they can to the clients. Tools and equipment would include computers, word processing software and other peripheral devices that make the medical transcriptionists more efficient in their line of work. The importance of medical transcriptions is that information can easily be relayed from one doctor to a specialist doctor or two organizations involved in health care of a patient such as the insurance companies.

Criteria of a Good Medical Transcriptionist

Being a medical transcriptionist requires a high degree of dedication and experience. It is a highly specialized skill therefore not just anyone can do this kind of job. An extensive knowledge about different medical terms is a must which can also be acquired through training and from on the job experience.

Although generally paid by the word or by the line, professional medical transcriptionists can earn a great deal of money, while often enjoying the benefits of working from home, as recent advances in computer and networking technologies have allowed medical transcriptionists to use the Internet for the uploading and downloading of information.

Although medical transcriptionists need extensive knowledge in the medical field, they do not need to have a University degree. It does not also require a lot of investment to start being one. Basically, what a person needs is to have the basic training and acquire good experience in an institution that specializes in medical transcription training.

In terms of medical transcription outsourcing, instead of the health care institution providing in-house transcription, they outsource this function to a 3rd party company. This way, they can focus on more important stuff related to health care and need not bother with other things such as medical transcription.

Through this, efficiency of transcription is also higher since people handling this function are trained as well as focused to only one thing – transcribing.

Chapter 23: Accounting Outsourcing: Delegating the Flow of Finances to Professionals in a Cost-efficient Way

Business is composed of a set of interrelated system that will ensure the smooth flow of business process and convert capital to revenue efficiently. It is important for a business owner to consider each component as if it is just the existing system inside the process. Thus, utmost importance and consideration must be given to each process component, which includes the accounting process.

That is why we have tax lawyers. That is why we have public accountants. That is why we have financial managers.

It is because of the accounting process.

It is the measurement and the disclosure of essential financial information that will help public accountants, financial managers, tax authorities, investors, and other decision-makers to effectively allocate their financial resources to each business process, thus maximizing the conversion of a business" working capital to huge revenues. Accounting involves processes in which important financial information of a particular business is recorded, summarized, evaluated, and interpreted. Furthermore, since money is one of the biggest factors that may affect the existence of a business in a certain market, accounting is given utmost attention and consideration at all times.

In accounting alone, there are several aspects that a business owner must consider. There you have the cost accounting, the cash-basis accounting, financial accounting, internal fund accounting, management accounting, project accounting, and others.

And the list continues to expand.

In other words, you might conclude that accounting is a serious and a critical matter that must be handled by a group of people who have the technical expertise in dealing with the accounting as well as financial issues. Realizing this reality, more and more business organizations hand the accounting aspects of their business process to third-party organizations, or most commonly known as accounting outsourcing.

Accounting outsourcing is considered to be one of the more effective management tool, thus many companies often incorporate outsourcing as one of their strategies in business planning.

As a matter of fact, the Outsourcing Institute reported that the concept of a CRO (Chief Resource Officer), a professional outsourcing executive manager, is widely-acceptable in larger corporate organizations. However, you need not to be a large corporation to benefit from accounting outsourcing. Even small and medium-sized enterprises can provide better service and produce high-quality products in a more cost-efficient way if they will outsource their non-core business processes, including the accounting aspect.

By decreasing the demands on your administrative personnel, you will be able to free them from additional responsibilities and they will be able to support areas directly to your sales, clients, and to the marketing task of your business.

Accounting outsourcing firms can execute your accounting and bookkeeping tasks in all frequencies (monthly, quarterly, and annually) or can supplement your present administrative staff to lessen the responsibility. Here is a summary of the services you can acquire from outsourcing your company's accounting process:

1. Preparing cash disbursement checks.
2. Preparing input credits and bank deposits.
3. Preparing company payroll.
4. Preparing tax deposits and bank reconciliation.
5. Preparing financial statements.
6. Preparing payroll tax returns.
7. Evaluation and review of financial results on different frequencies.

With accounting outsourcing, you will be able to see the benefits of having a cost-efficient business operation. With your accounting process at the hands of outsourcing professionals, you can focus to the core of your business and convert every cent of your working capital into hundreds to thousands of dollars in generated revenues and profits.

Chapter 24: A Closer Look at Recruitment Process Outsourcing

The growing scarcity of talent around the world and its potential effect on global productivity continues to be a problem for various businesses, governments and private individuals. Thanks to recruitment process outsourcing (RPO), companies can now trim down the resources they need to devote to hiring so that more time and effort can be concentrated on core competencies.

What is RPO?

RPO is a type of business process outsourcing wherein a company –either big or small– turns over all or a fraction of its recruitment functions to a service provider. Based on the statement released by the RPO Association, recruitment process outsourcing takes place when an external provider operates as the company's internal hiring department for all or a portion of its job openings.

RPO service providers deal with all of the recruitment steps from the profiling to the reception of newly hired employees. A well-managed RPO will also increase the company's recruitment time, improve the quality of the applicant pool, make demonstrable metrics available, drive down overheads and enhance legislative compliance.

Alternatively, intermittent recruitment support such as transitory, contingency and decision-making search services is more comparable to co-sourcing, out-tasking, or simply sourcing. In this case in point, the external service provider is the source of specific types of hiring functions.

The major difference between recruitment process outsourcing and other kinds of recruitment lies in the fact that the first assumes possession of the process while the latter is merely part of the process being dealt with by the company that purchases their services.

The Benefits

Promoters of RPO assert that the solution tenders enhancement in quality, service, speed and costs. In addition to that, the cost benefits that a company acquires because of business growth; also known as economies of scale, allows them to offer staffing processes at a much lower expenditure while economies of scope makes it possible for them to function as first-rate specialists. Economies of both scale and scope are believed to arise out of a bigger team of recruiters, records of applicant resumes, and venture in recruitment networks and tools.

Recruitment process outsourcing solutions are also deemed to alter preset investment costs into flexible overheads that oscillate together with fluctuations in recruitment activity. Businesses may pay via transaction instead of by team member, therefore staying away from under-use or imposing costly discharge of recruitment personnel when activity is sluggish.

The Drawbacks

If a business does not succeed in defining its overall recruitment tactics and hiring goals, then any recruitment plan have a tendency to fall short in meeting the company's requirements. This is particularly true for outsourced services such as RPO. It may only be successful in the context of a well-delineated business and recruitment strategy.

Like any program, a company ought to supervise its RPO operations. It must make preliminary guidance available, as well as continuous monitoring, in order to ensure the preferred outcome. On the whole, giving directions to external activities can exhibit a considerable challenge concerning management. Outsourcing of business processes may be unsuccessful or demonstrate an inadequate organizational fit. Thus, an inappropriately executed RPO could also lead to diminished recruitment efficiency.

Another possible drawback of recruitment process outsourcing involves an over-sized expenditure meant for staffing transactions. In other words, the total sum could amount to more than the actual costs of an in-house recruitment division.

Chapter 25: Human Resource Outsourcing Services: Providing Experts for your Company

Do you lack experts and time in your company to get the job done? If you do, then you need to outsource human resource tasks to an outside company. This means that you need to hire a company to do some of the job your company has to do in order for profit to grow.

It is a fact that some of the jobs that you need to do require professionals. However, if you hire a professional in your company, it will usually be too expensive and will take a lot of time. If you outsource it to outsourcing companies and freelancers, you will be saving a lot of money in terms of salaries.

Human resource tasks, such as payrolls, benefits administration, business processes and employee management are now outsourced to other companies, usually offshore, in order to save on business expenses. Human resource outsourcing is now becoming a booming business in other countries, such as China, Philippines, India and other developing countries. They offer cheap and quality services for companies who are outsourcing human resources.

Since outsourcing saves a lot of money, your company will be able to cut costs in human resource jobs. Also, there are a lot of professionals in these developing countries that are competent and are qualified to do your human resources jobs. They will be able to provide you with quality services at a very competitive price.

Another great thing about outsourcing your human resources jobs is that it will allow your company to focus on more important factors than human resources. It will effectively let you manage your company's priorities more efficiently.

Your company will also be able to save a lot of money on building your own in-house human resource department. This is because the outsourcing companies already have the technology and you do not have to invest a lot of money by developing your own in-house human resources department. The outsourcing company will be the one to provide the technology for you. They will only charge you with the services they do.

However, with all the advantages that human resource outsourcing can provide you, there will always be some disadvantages.

Since you will be letting other companies handle your human resources jobs, you will be providing sensitive information to them. Make sure that the outsourcing services you hire has a strong organization that will be able to keep your company's information, whatever it is, confidential.

Another disadvantage is that when you outsource your human resource department, you will be directing your clients to the outsourcing company.

This means that you will be losing direct communication with your clients and it might weaken your relationship with your clients and potential clients. Because of this, you have to make sure that the quality of the outsourcing company's services remains at par with your standards.

These are the things you should remember when you are considering to outsource your human resources department. Keeping all of these in mind will ensure quality in the services of the outsourcing company.

So, if you need outsourcing as a growth engine or a way to access human resource technology without spending a lot of money on technology or reduce administrative overheads in order for your company to focus on more important issues, you should consider outsourcing as a great tool for your company. Always remember that strategic roles of your company should always be kept in-house.

Chapter 26: Human Resource Outsourcing: the fundamentals

For reasons of having no time and resources to manage human resource functions, companies usually resort to HR outsourcing. It is a cost-effective way of managing human resource functions without having to resort to employing personnel for an in-house HR staff.

There are a lot of benefits that businesses can gain from outsourcing HR tasks. One of the most appealing benefits is the ability of a company to focus on their core business activities while still having effective HR policies.

Is HR Outsourcing for Everybody

Given that HR outsourcing is beneficial, unfortunately it is not for everybody. There are pros and cons in outsourcing and it all depends on the situation of a company. To better assess whether HR outsourcing is right for you here is a guide:

1. Do you feel comfortable letting other people (outside of the company) take care of the HR functions? There are people who just can't trust outsiders to handle any of the company's functions most often because of trust issues. This kind of thinking however is very much acceptable since it is possible that there are firms that take advantage of their position.

2. Does the company have enough resources to take care of HR functions? If a company has the ability to handle their own HR functions, then there is no need to outsource. This is most especially true in big companies. But if you lack the resources and HR representatives to do the job effectively, then you may opt to go for HR outsourcing.

3. Which is more costly? It should be evaluated whether outsourcing is more cost-effective than having your own staff for the HR functions. It is true that HR outsourcing usually costs less but there are some situations wherein this is not the case.

How to Choose an HR Firm

When you have decided to go for HR outsourcing, you need to choose wisely which HR firm to choose to avoid any complications in future.

Companies have different criteria when choosing HR firms. Some decide basing on costs, some companies look for companies that are committed to quality and there are companies that are strict on looking for both cost efficiency and quality.

When choosing an HR firm, you may want to consider these following criteria:
First, you need to know the firm's offered services.

Second, you need to know the level of expertise it has in terms of your line of business.

Third, you should assess the firm's general HR experience. Fourth, there is a need to know there available resources.

And last but not the least; you need to be informed how flexible the contracts are.

An HR firm whether outsourced or in-house is considered as an extension of the company so you need to have one that fits your image. That is why you also need to consider the kind of HR firm you want to hire. An HR firm specializing in law firms and financial institutions may not match your new business. It is possible that it will not be able to know and understand your needs.

Types of HR Firms

There are basically two types of HR firms: Professional Employer Organization (PEO) and Hybrid HR firm.

Professional Employer Organization is for companies who are comfortable with handing over the whole HR functions to a 3rd party organization. However, if you have any inhibitions about letting somebody else take care of the HR functions, then you may opt to go for the Hybrid.

Chapter 27: Business Outsourcing and Verifying Employees

When you decide upon business outsourcing for project needs it is important to verify who the people are who will be working in your business. You should verify the employees as you would your own.

If you run backgrounds tests on your employees, then you should do the same with an outsourcing business's employees.

It will be hard for you to demand that outsourcing employees agree to a background check or a drug test. What you can do is use only a company who will provide the proof to you the people are acceptable. You should get a name of every person who will be entering your business working on the project.

Sometimes when there are a lot of people entering the business from an outsourced company it can be confusing who is with the company and who is in the building without authorization.

Be sure you know each employee who works for the outsourced company and provide them with temporary badges to wear. This way, anyone who is not wearing one of the temporary badges can be questioned with reason.

Your employees have a right to feel safe at their place of work. You cannot bring in people who have dangerous backgrounds to work on an outsourced project for you.

You should verify all of the provided information and know every person who will be working on an outsourced project. All of these employees from the business outsourcing company should be properly introduced to your staff so everyone feels comfortable with the people walking through the halls.

Chapter 28: Do you Compromise Quality with Outsourcing?

The simple answer to this question is yes, and no and maybe. Well, maybe it is not such a simple answer because it is a particularly loaded question. The subject of outsourcing is a very sensitive issue for many. There are some who believe that outsourcing, whether it is overseas or domestic, is taking jobs away from qualified individuals while others who are profiting from outsourcing are firm advocates for the practice. This book will take a look at outsourcing and will examine scenarios when quality is compromised as well as scenarios when quality is not compromised.

What is Outsourcing?

For those who are still confused about what outsourcing entails, this chapter will explain the issue. In its most basic form, outsourcing is employing an individual outside of the work organization to perform specific tasks for monetary compensation. Outsourcing can be done on a per project basis, for a set period of time or on an ongoing basis for an undetermined period of time.

For many the word outsourcing has a very negative connotation. When they think of outsourcing, they picture underage employees in third world countries working for salaries which would be paltry by our standards. However, outsourcing has evolved so much and no longer resembles this stereotype.

In fact many outsourcing takes place domestically by savvy entrepreneurs who market their abilities as an independent contractor rather than toiling away in corporate America. These individuals, enjoy their quality of life, negotiate fair compensation for their work and accept or decline work at their own will. Furthermore these individuals are often highly qualified for the positions they accept and are capable of producing work of a high standard.

When Outsourcing Compromises Quality

The simplest answer to this question is quality is compromised when price becomes the sole governing factor in selecting a candidate to complete the outsourced task. Of course this answer is not completely accurate because the truth is there are very educated and skilled employees overseas who are fully capable of completing tasks just as well as those living in this country and often for a much lower price. However, when only domestic candidates are being considered and price is the governing factor, quality is often compromised as it is very rare that the most qualified candidate is also the candidate with the lowest rates.

However, it is very common for an individual or a business to allow price to become more important than quality of work. When this happens quality is often compromised for the sake of a larger profit. An example of this is seen regularly on websites where outsourcing projects are listed and potential applicants submit their bids for these projects. Many who utilize these websites routinely select the lowest bidder without regard for the qualifications of the bidder. In most cases these individuals find they make a costly mistake when the work they receive is inadequate.

When Outsourcing does not Compromise Quality

Outsourcing does not always compromise quality. In fact in many cases outsourcing is not only the most affordable option but also provides the most qualified candidates. One way to avoid the pitfalls of having quality compromised by outsourcing is to carefully screen candidates before making a decision. This process should be taken just as seriously as hiring a full time employee because the work of the individual will reflect on you as an individual or your business. If due diligence is given to selecting the right candidate it is not likely that quality will be compromised.

When outsourcing work to an individual it is important to request detailed information regarding their qualifications and to verify all information supplied. Examples of information to request include:
1. Previous work history.
2. Relevant work experiences.
3. Explanation of qualifications.

Additionally, it is wise to ask for both business and personal references. These references should all be contacted and questioned about the work ethic and personal integrity of the individual.

Chapter 29: Request for Proposal when Business Outsourcing and its Benefits

A Request for Proposal (RFP) is something you write when you are looking for an outsourcing company to complete a project for you.

There are many benefits to writing an RFP you should know before you begin.

The primary purpose of an RFP is to inform suppliers that your company is looking for business outsourcing and it encourages these companies to make their best effort in meeting your requirements.

In an RFP for business outsourcing you will be specific to the products you would like to use in your project.

For instance, if you want to upgrade your file servers and you would like to use IBM Blade servers then you should specify this requirement.

The more specific you are with your requirements and your budget, the better bids you will receive.

An RFP also forces suppliers to be realistic and factual identify your requirements when they come back with an offer on your RFP.

It also allows for a larger response to your request for business outsourcing.

It also gives you the opportunity to let the suppliers know that the process of selection is competitive.

A closed bid selection is the best way to go when you are looking at suppliers bids on your project. This way, it doesn't allow a business outsourcing company to underbid another company for the project.

You should never tell a company what another company bid on the project and give them the opportunity. The entire selection process should be fair to all of the companies.

The best way to find a business outsourcing company is to write a Request for Proposal for the project and include detailed requirements for the project.

Chapter 30: A Look at Business Process Outsourcing in China

China is one of the leading countries that provide services in the software outsourcing market. Its outsourcing services market became more rational and steady in 2006, reaching 1.43 billion USD and has been growing rapidly in the international market with a year to year growth of 55.4%, which is 10% more than last year.

To grow up with an international market in software outsourcing industries, many capital firms are giving a boost to the development of software outsourcing. On the other hand, cooperation with the multinational market by the domestic software outsourcing service providers is also occurring. Also, human resource, opening customer services and customer resources as well as market environment are playing their part in the future development of the software market. Also Japanese service enterprises are expanding in China at an expedited pace.

In 2006-2007, the annual report on Chinas software outsourcing market by CCID was submitted that helped service providers, investors, capital firms and government agencies to grasp the opportunities in boosting the software outsourcing market. It is also predicted that china software market will increase rapidly with the estimated annual growth rate of 50 percent from 2005 to 2011. Thus the rapid growth of China's software outsourcing service market is raking profits internationally in the outsourcing market. Currently, the potential with the estimate annual rate of 50% which is 10% more than last year has been maintained in the Chinese software outsourcing industry that nevertheless shares a small proportion globally.

Software business with Japan has grown 30 percent since 1996, where the country is doing business of about a 50 million. Since 2006 China has captured more than 60% of the Japanese software outsourcing market and this has been helping China make its mark globally. Chinas software industry has been growing faster since trading with Japan. In addition, the plus point could also be that the Japanese firms prefer China for the outsourcing market because they are close neighbours and have similar cultural backgrounds.

This has increased the overall demand as well since European and US companies have been enlarging their cooperation and trade with China and this has the same fallout effect of nurturing the image of the Chinese software outsourcing industry.

Analyzing the rapid growth in providing the services in the field of software outsourcing market, Japanese outsourcers are much more co operative in providing or dealing with their Chinese partners, it helps in boosting globally the software service market.

Chapter 31: How Business Process Outsourcing Fares in India Today

The act of contracting business process functions to a third party, more commonly known as business process outsourcing or BPO is an increasingly popular trend. Today, many of the world's biggest companies have outsourced some of their activities, and most of them find their way to the cities of India. Business Process Outsourcing in India: The BPO industry in India continues to grow. Now known as 'the back office of the world", India is home to outsourcing firms of numerous Fortune 500 and FTSE 100 companies.

In the 1980's, a number of European airlines had established back offices in India, and this arguably built the roots of what's now one of the world's most active business process outsourcing industries.

Other companies soon followed. In the same decade, American Express brought over its Japan-Asia Pacific branch into New Delhi. In the 1990's, General Electrics also came to set up its back office in India. Other well-known corporations that had outsourced their various business needs to India include Motorola, Standards Chartered Bank, Yahoo, Dell, Cisco, and Delta Air Lines.

Cities with high BPO activity include New Delhi, the country's capital, Chennai, and Bangalore. Due to increasing infrastructure costs however, other cities are slowly being developed to match the resources provided by Tier I cities. Tier II cities include Jaipur, Mysore, and Kochi.

Advantages of Business Outsourcing in India There are various benefits that companies can enjoy if they choose to outsource several of their activities to India. Human Resources Labour is comparatively cheaper in India than in Western regions like the United States and key cities in Europe. The Indian labour force is also well-educated and with varying skills and talents. Neither does it hurt that Indians had long been educated to speak English.

Pioneers in Software Development India is one of the world's pioneers in software development. Multinational IT firms would not find it terribly difficult to procure competent resources for their needs in India.

Technology and Infrastructure: The country's government is very much aware of the economic benefits offered by the growing BPO industry. As such, they have been more than willing in recent years to improve infrastructure and technology in order to make their cities well-equipped to handle just about any call centre need of multinational companies.

Problems Encountered by the Business Process Outsourcing Industry in India Of course, the BPO industry, just like other industries, is not free from problems. One major problem is the high rate of attrition. Many BPO firms are keen on addressing the high rate of attrition in their operations. There are various reasons why many employees are choosing to leave their relatively high-paid jobs.

Many jobs in the BPO sector require employees to work at night and while they are certainly well-compensated for their efforts, this does not negate the fact that they did have to stay up late for work and suffer possible health problems due to their unusual work schedule.

Stress and pressure during work is not something to scoff at either, and this is another reason why people prefer to leave their jobs in the BPO industry.

Business Process Outsourcing in India Today Recent news has predicted India to generate more than 8 million jobs over the next decade from the BPO industry alone. One-fourth of this figure will be immediately taken up by Tier II and III cities in India.

Today, ninety percent of the BPO industry's labour force is situated in the country's top seven BPO and ITO cities. This however has produced problems like oversubscribed universities, rising infrastructure costs, and overburdened roads.

It is the country's hope that Tier II and III cities will soon be able to provide the requisite resources so as not to put the growth opportunity in BPO to waste.

Chapter 32: Business Outsourcing Contracts

When you consider business outsourcing it is important to draw up a contractual agreement for you and the outsourcing company to sign.

This agreement will define the project in full including items such as the time line, budget, people, and more. When you decide on a business for outsourcing it is important to draw up a contract. The contract will spell out all of your expectations to the project and what the role of the company and their employees will be.

This gives you the opportunity to hold the company accountable for the work you are asking to be done. When you sign a contractual agreement for business outsourcing the contract will specify the time frame of the project and set a timeline.

The timeline will set milestones during the project and specify each with an expected completion date. In addition, many contractual agreements will specify percentages of payment according to the completion of each set milestone.

If the completion or the milestone is not met on the expected date, a stipulation may be defined on the contractual agreement also.

The contract signed between you and a business outsourcing company will define the budget of the project and what the company has agreed to do the project for.

If the company has underbid the project, then they must pay the excess funds to complete the project. It is not your responsibility if the company underbids and the contract should be clear on this.

This includes the amount of hours it takes for completion of the project. If the company promised the project would be completed in a certain amount of hours and it is not then their staff will be working for free until the project is completed.

You must sign a contractual agreement along with the business outsourcing company you are hiring. This is to protect the company and the funds you have for the project.

Chapter 33: Arguments for Keeping Jobs within the Borders

If you have called a company's customer service call centre or a computer manufacturer's tech support department lately, you probably have had the "joy" of experiencing outsourcing for yourself.

The inefficiency of non-native English speakers as tech support personnel is astounding; however, corporate management across the US and UK feel the money saved in salaries by sending jobs to south-east Asia outweighs the nose-dive in customer satisfaction ratings.

Forrester Research predicts that by 2015 at least 3.3 million white-collar jobs ($136 billion in wage earnings) will be outsourced outside the US and UK. As US consumers demand lower prices for goods and services while seeking higher and higher salaries, corporate America is caught in the squeeze and has sought a solution outside the borders of the US. But what if there is a solution closer to home – say in Arkansas?

Outsourcing to rural America may be a win-win solution for the growing problem of rising salaries and demand for lower cost goods. With the cost of living up to one third lower in rural areas of the US compared to major metropolitan areas such as San Francisco or New York, salaries are lower and talent is more abundant. IT salaries in rural America can be as much as 40% lower than in large metro areas, offset by lower costs of living. It makes sense to send customer service and IT work to underemployed workers in areas such as North Carolina and New Mexico.

What types of jobs might be prime targets for rural outsourcing? Most IT positions from software developers to project managers can be sent to rural America as can most jobs that have a home-based element. Customer service centres are being moved out further from urban areas to take advantage of available labour and native speakers of English. Outsourcing within the borders means broader opportunities for executives and managers who wish to opt out of the urban lifestyle and settle in smaller towns that provide safer environments with less stress. Taking a job in a rural area may mean a 20% pay cut but usually the lower cost of living offsets the cut, and may actually reduce expenses such as gas and food costs.

It pays to investigate small town opportunities which, granted won't have as many opportunities available as the big metro areas, but the upside is you will also have a lot less competition. For example, McKesson Corporation, a large pharmaceutical distributor, relocated a primary data centre from San Francisco to Iowa and saved an estimated $10 million in annual salary costs. Besides the salary cost benefit, there are other benefits to keeping the work at home including friendly time zone spans, cultural understanding, common language, and preserving the tax base. The political and economic benefits cannot be underestimated, either. Nashville, Tennessee provided Dell Computer with tax incentives to locate a manufacturing and customer service location in their area.

Jennifer Daly a native of Manchester, Tennessee, a small town of approximately 20,000 people says, "Nearly all the top 10% of my high school graduating class have left the area. We all went to college and got engineering, computer, or education degrees but could not remain at home because there just weren't any jobs here. It is too bad. This is a great town to raise a family."

With the post-9/11 era of urban flight, bringing the white collar jobs to small town America is a growing trend. Professionals in rural areas are as well-educated as their urban colleagues and are not as burdened with high housing costs and other cost of living items. Bringing the jobs to them that would otherwise be sent to India, Malaysia, or China benefits everyone in terms of cost savings and better customer service.

And I would also suggest that the UK Government look at doing the same. We have North of England, Scotland and Wales where most of the jobs going offshore can be located to.

Chapter 34: The Pros and Cons of Outsourcing your Business Process

Outsourcing is defined as the relinquishing of certain duties and tasks to an outside company or individual. Outsourcing is becoming a common business practice in today's society. Outsourcing enables many business owners to continue their operations, but at reduced costs. With that in mind, it is important to know that outsourcing is not right for all businesses. Before making the decision to outsource your business process tasks, it is advised that you examine the pros and cons of doing so.

As for the pros or plus sides to outsourcing your business process duties and tasks, you will find that there are a number of them. Perhaps, the biggest pro to business process outsourcing is the money you are able to save.

Outsourcing a number of your needed tasks can actually save you a considerable amount of money, especially overtime. Business owners who make the decision to outsource to other countries, such as India, are able to save the most money, due to lower living wages. With that in mind, even if you use outsourced workers from the United States or UK, the cost should be lower than hiring an in-house employee. This is because you can hire all workers as contract workers, instead of in-house workers. This should save you money on healthcare and other benefits.

Another pro or plus side to outsourcing business process duties is one that is best for small to medium sized business owners. This is because outsourced work is often done offsite; either in a call centre or at the home of a home based worker. This can work out to your advantage if you are interested in closing down your office. For example, if you run a dental office, but you are interested in taking a vacation or simply just leaving work early a few days a month, outsourcing enables you to do so without any complications. Having an offsite office manager enables you to leave your office without having to worry about who is left behind or if your office will be properly locked up. This comfort and peace of mind is nice for many.

Although there are a number of pros or plus sides to outsourcing your business process duties, it is also important to focus on the cons or downsides as well.
One of those cons or downsides is what outsourcing can do to your local economy. Although one outsourced worker may not make a huge difference on your local economy and local residents searching for a job, it is important to remember that outsourcing is becoming a common practice for many business owners. This often leaves fewer jobs for local residents. These are the same local residents that are likely to support your business and bring you income. With that in mind, it is also important to examine your role as a business owner; your goal is to make money. Still, you may want to focus on this

important fact, especially if you would lay off a full-time worker of yours to outsource their duties.

It is also important to remember that not all business process duties can be outsourced. As you likely already know, office managers perform a wide range of tasks. These tasks may include supervising other office personnel. This supervision may not be possible with an outsourced office manager. If your office manager would be responsible for overseeing other office staff members, it may be best for you to hire an in-house office manager, as opposed to outsourcing. If cost is a concern of yours, you may want to offer one of your secretaries or other staff members the chance to supervise, for a small increase in pay.

The pros and cons outlined above are just a few of the many that you will want to take into consideration, when determining if your business process tasks can be or should be outsourced.

As a reminder, outsourcing can save many business owners money, but it may not be in your best interest or the best interest of your company.

Chapter 35: Conclusion

The business process involves a lot of things. It will involve every aspect of your company in order to let your company operate smoothly and efficiently. It will involve business tasks, such as marketing, payrolls, help desks, management, human resources and more.

In the past, handling all these can be easy. But because of the growing demands in businesses today, you have to consider that it will be difficult for your company to cope up with today's competitiveness in the business world. Your company should maximize its resources in order to remain competitive with other companies.

This would be impossible or very expensive if you handle every business process involved. This is why many companies are now considering outsourcing their business process.

Business process outsourcing is one of the most popular and the most cost-efficient business solution that you can ever make. By contracting other companies to do a specific business task, you will be taking off extra work involved in your company and focus more on important aspects in running your business.

For example, making payrolls can be time consuming. It will involve computation of salaries of every employees and it will also involve taxes. You can hire your own employees to do the payroll for you. But, this will only add to the expenses that your company is making. Your target would be to decrease overall expense in your company. So, in order to save money, you have to outsource this particular business process to companies that accepts outsourcing.

Another example would be the help desk. Every company that manufactures products needs one. This particular business process is a way to communicate with your clients and know about their feedback in your products and it is also a way to assist your clients in case they encounter difficulty with your product. Creating a help desk department may prove to be too costly. It will involve everything from hiring additional employees and purchasing all the necessary tools you need to create an efficient and working help desk.

Today, there are available call centre companies that will be able to provide a help desk for you. They will be the one who will answer your calls and generate reports regarding each caller and providing the reports for your company.

Companies regularly outsource their business process offshore, particularly to developing countries filled with qualified and talented individuals, such as China, Philippines, Mexico and India. These countries offer good quality services for your business process and they charge a very cheap rate for these services.

By outsourcing your company's business process or some of your company's business process, your company will be able to utilize its facilities to its maximum potential.

Through business process outsourcing you will be able to cut some operational costs and at the same time, let your company focus more on important factors in running your own business.

These are the reasons why you should consider outsourcing your business process to offshore companies.

Always keep in mind that you should first check the quality of an offshore outsourcing company first before you sign the contract in order to be sure that you will be getting your money's worth. Remember this and it will pave the way to make your company the best in the industry.

Good Luck!